EDGE BOOKS™

DRAWING COOL STUFF

HOW TO DRAW DISGUSTING ALIENS

by Aaron Sautter

illustrated by Bob Lentz

Capstone press®

Mankato, Minnesota

Edge Books are published by Capstone Press,
151 Good Counsel Drive, P.O. Box 669, Mankato, Minnesota 56002.
www.capstonepress.com

Library of Congress Cataloging-in-Publication Data
Sautter, Aaron.
    How to draw disgusting aliens / by Aaron Sautter; illustrated by Bob Lentz.
    p. cm.—(Edge books. Drawing cool stuff)
    Summary: "Lively text and fun illustrations describe how to draw disgusting
aliens"—Provided by publisher.
    Includes bibliographical references and index.
    ISBN–13: 978-1-4296-0075-0 (hardcover)
    ISBN–10: 1-4296-0075-6 (hardcover)
    1. Life on other planets in art—Juvenile literature. 2. Drawing—Technique—
Juvenile literature. I. Lentz, Bob. II. Title. III. Series.
NC825.O9S28 2008
743'.89576839—dc22   2007003451

Credits
Jason Knudson, set designer

1 2 3 4 5 6 12 11 10 09 08 07

TABLE OF CONTENTS

WELCOME!

You probably picked this book because you love the gruesome, creepy aliens you see in movies and TV shows. Or maybe you picked it because you like to draw. Whatever the reason, get ready to dive into the world of disgusting aliens!

Aliens can be any shape or size you can imagine. Some might have slimy tentacles or razor-sharp teeth. Others might look fuzzy and cute but are really very dangerous. Whatever they might look like—aliens are out of this world!

This book is just a starting point. Once you've learned how to draw the different slimy, disgusting aliens in this book, you can start drawing your own. Let your imagination run wild, and see what sort of nasty creatures you can create!

To get started, you'll need some supplies:

1. First you'll need drawing paper. Any type of blank, unlined paper will do.

2. Pencils are the easiest to use for your drawing projects. Make sure you have plenty of them.

3. You have to keep your pencils sharp to make clean lines. Keep a pencil sharpener close by. You'll use it a lot.

4. As you practice drawing, you'll need a good eraser. Pencil erasers wear out very fast. Get a rubber or kneaded eraser. You'll be glad you did.

5. When your drawing is finished, you can trace over it with a black ink pen or thin felt-tip marker. The dark lines will really make your work stand out.

6. If you decide to color your drawings, colored pencils and markers usually work best. You can also use colored pencils to shade your drawings and make them more lifelike.

VOGGLES

Voggles are some of the weirdest aliens you'll ever see. Their special eye antennas let each Voggle see what all other Voggles see. This makes Voggles the best security guards around for the Helix Galactic Bank.

After drawing this alien, try giving him a crazy, weird body to match his head!

STEP 1

STEP 2

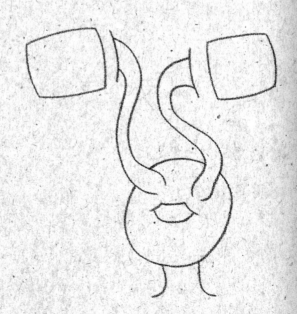

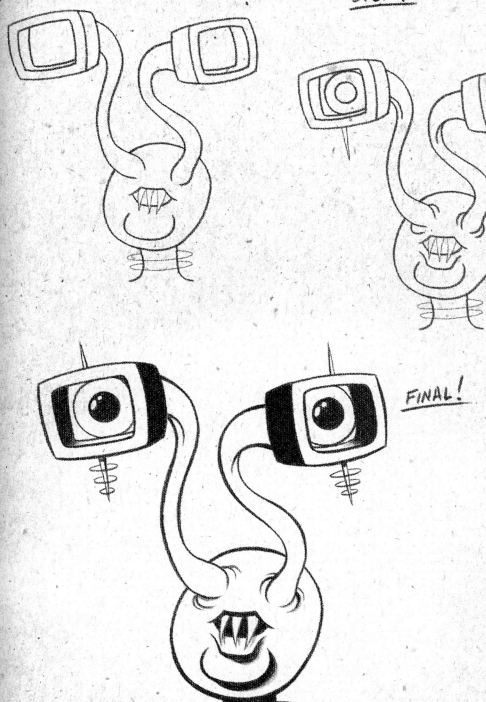

FINAL!

SKRAWKS

The Skrawk people have been involved in galactic politics for hundreds of years. They think every person's opinion is important. Skrawks who aren't involved with politics usually work as lawyers or for the Galactic Peace Corps.

STEP 1

When you're done drawing this strange alien, try giving him a new suit or a snazzy Peace Corps uniform!

STEP 2

STEP 3

STEP 4

FINAL!

9

THE GIANT BLORP

If you're ever on the planet Tantil-3, watch out for the Giant Blorp! At first it seems like a gentle snail-like creature. But don't get too close! If the Blorp smells you, it'll grab you with its sticky tongue tentacles and gobble you up for breakfast!

After drawing this picture, try giving the Giant Blorp even more wild and crazy tongue tentacles!

STEP 1

STEP 2

STEP 3

STEP 4

FINAL!

11

SNALIDS

Anelid Prime is home to a dangerous alien race. Snalids are slippery creatures with mouths full of razor-sharp teeth. The Snalid queen sent out thousands of Snalid soldiers to bring back food for her colony. Don't let these things get near you, or you might become their next tasty snack!

When you're done drawing this alien, try a swarm of them getting ready to attack!

STEP 1

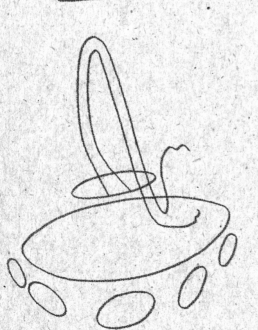

STEP 2

STEP 3

STEP 4

FINAL!

13

GORAXIANS

Goraxians are brutal warriors. They love to fight, and their micro-ray guns are deadly in battle. But if they lose radio contact with the Goraxian commander, they simply stop in place. If you're in a fight with a Goraxian, try to break off his antenna—it might be your only chance!

Try drawing the Goraxian commander! You can give him some special armor or a radio communicator.

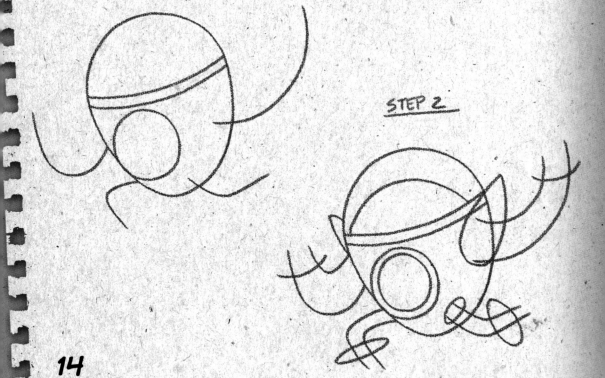

STEP 1

STEP 2

STEP 3

STEP 4

FINAL!

15

CYCLOPOIDS

Cyclopoids might look weird, but they are some of the galaxy's best pilots. Their sharp vision and lightning-quick reflexes help them avoid almost any obstacle in space. If you ever need to fly through an asteroid field, be sure to hire a Cyclopoid!

After drawing this alien, try creating a weird, wacky-looking creature of your own!

STEP 1

STEP 2

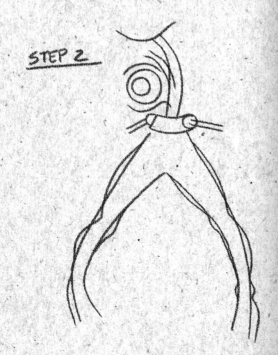

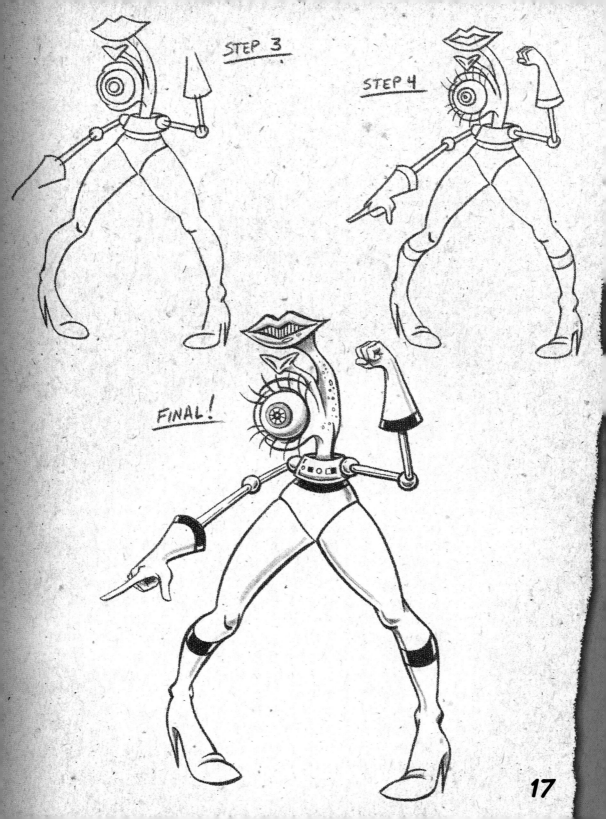

STEP 3

STEP 4

FINAL!

17

JAMBO WHELON

Jambo Whelon was a powerful crime lord from the planet Khoroth. He created the Cyber League to gather vast wealth. But League rebels forced Jambo into hiding. Luckily, his cybernetic leg and other implants help him hide from those who want to make him disappear permanently.

After you've finished this drawing, try giving Jambo even more cybernetic body parts!

STEP 1

STEP 2

STEP 3

STEP 4

FINAL!

19

THE SIX-LEGGED SKREETCH

Few horrors are as terrifying as the Six-Legged Skreetch. Its name comes from the piercing shriek it uses to paralyze its prey. And its razor-sharp claws can rip through any armor. There's only one thing to do if you see one of these—RUN!

STEP 1

When you're done with this drawing, try giving the Skreetch more teeth or even bigger claws!

STEP 2

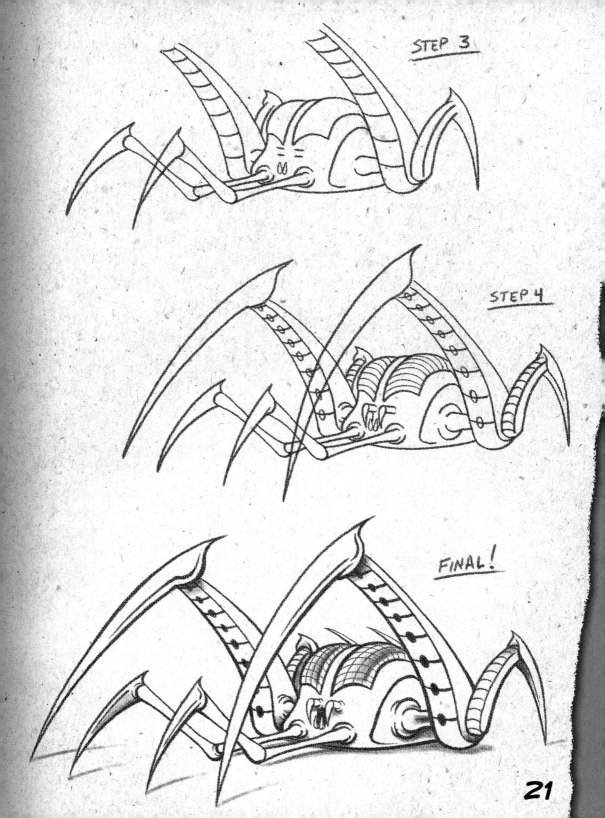

STEP 3

STEP 4

FINAL!

21

GRULDAN GLIDERS

The planet Gruldan is home to one of the galaxy's fiercest predators. The Gruldan Glider's dragonlike wings make it an excellent flyer. It hunts with heat-vision, and it kills its prey with venom sprayed from its tongue. You don't want to see one of these flying overhead!

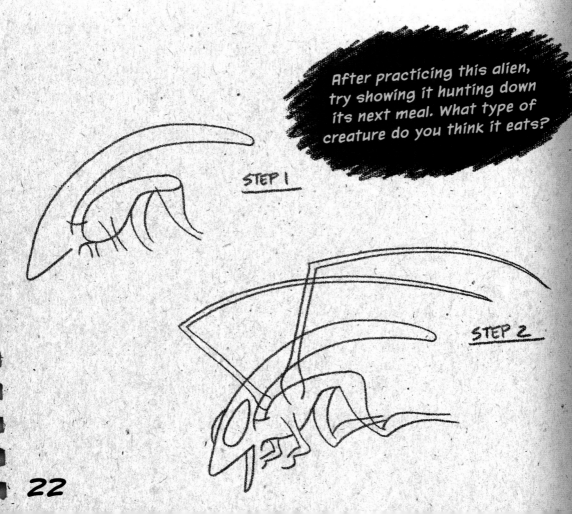

After practicing this alien, try showing it hunting down its next meal. What type of creature do you think it eats?

STEP 1

STEP 2

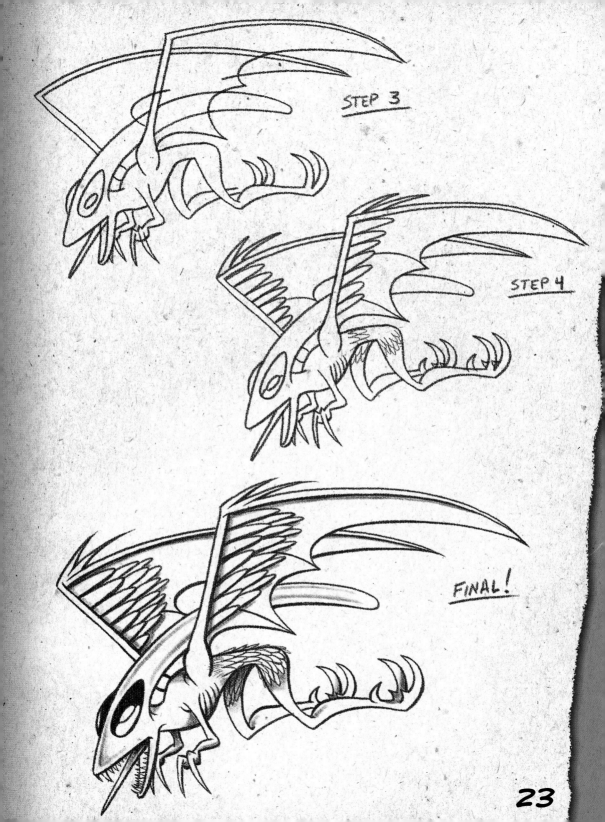

STEP 3

STEP 4

FINAL!

23

THE PHLOREEN

The Phloreen are huge creatures that ate every plant on their home world. Now they are known as the Harvesters. They travel from planet to planet taking every green plant they find. Hopefully they will never find your planet. If they do, it might end up a dead world like countless others the Harvesters have left behind.

After practicing this giant alien, try creating your own. What kinds of huge creatures can you imagine?

STEP 1

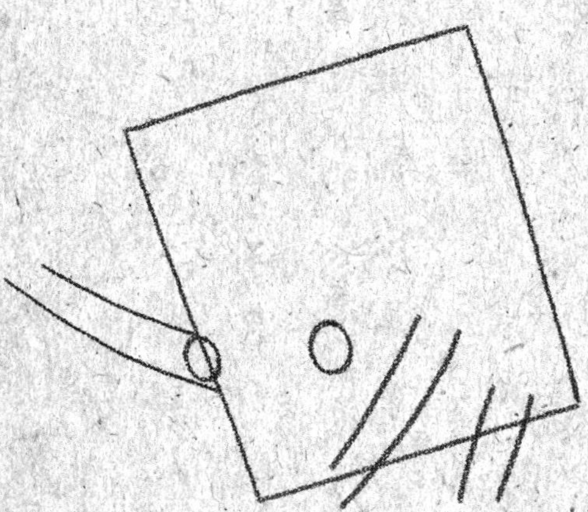

STEP 2

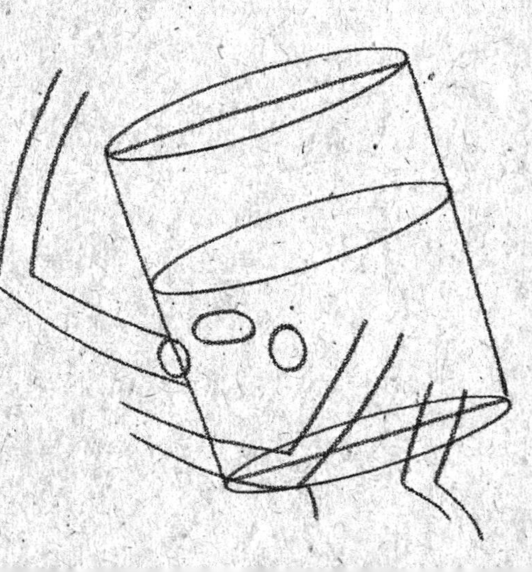

24

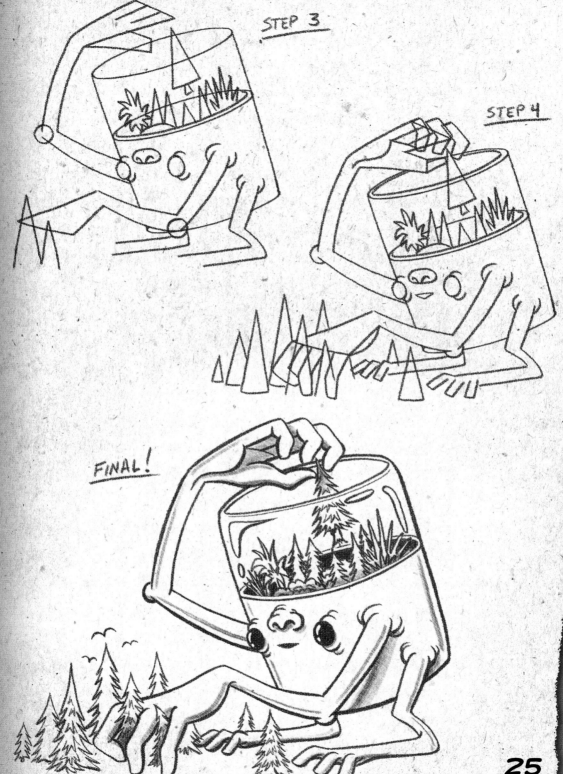

STEP 3

STEP 4

FINAL!

BATTLE ROYALE!

Thydians and Pongos have fought for control of the planet Darhoon for many generations. But neither side can win. A Thydian's scaly hide and sharp pincers are matched by a Pongo's electro-staff and natural quickness. Perhaps one day they'll realize the planet's resources can be shared, and they can finally live in peace.

When you've mastered this drawing, try it again with the aliens in different battle poses!

STEP 1

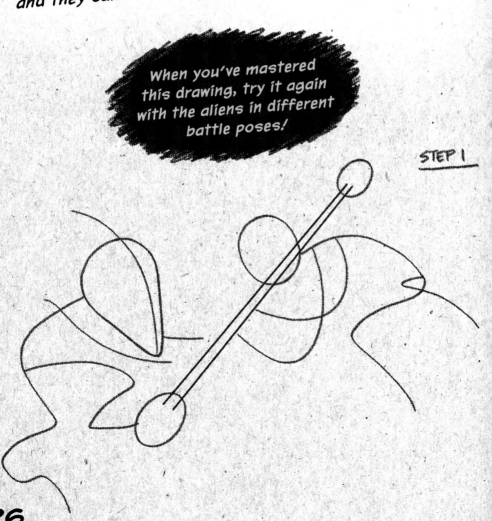

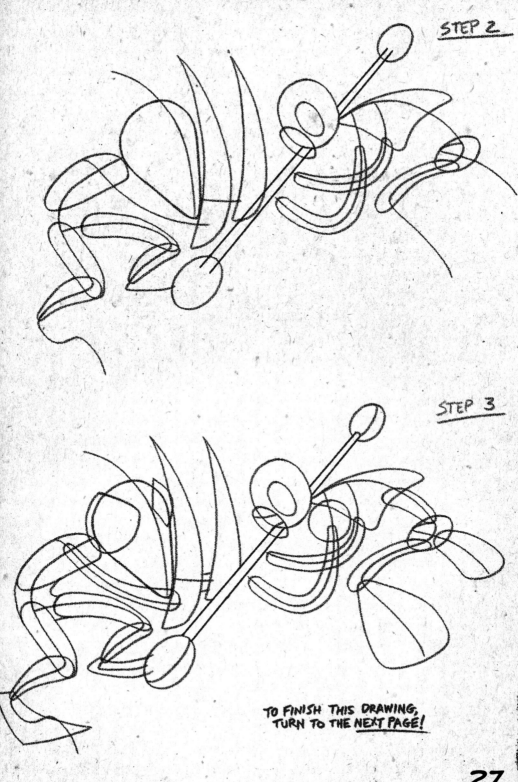

TO FINISH THIS DRAWING,
TURN TO THE NEXT PAGE!

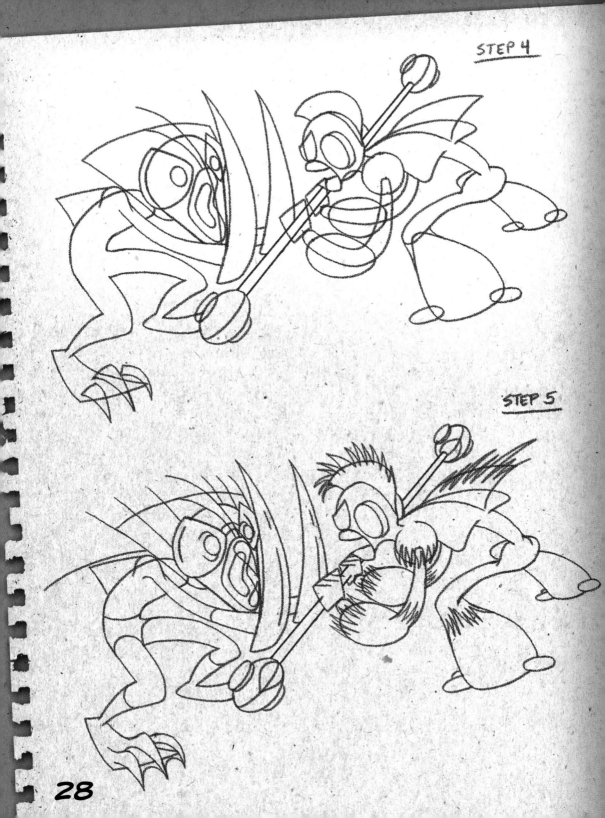

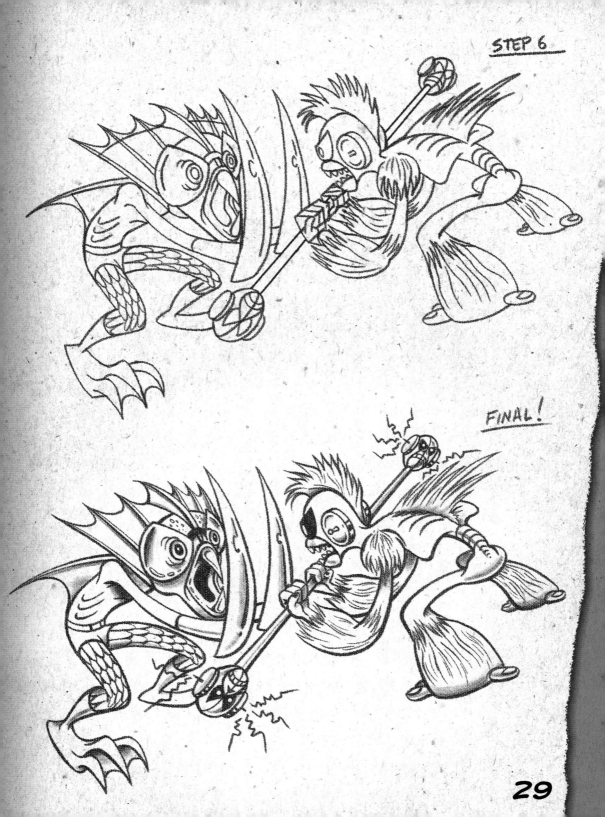

FINAL!

GLOSSARY

colony (KOL-uh-nee)—a large group of animals or creatures that live together in the same area

cybernetic (SYE-bur-net-ik)—something that is artificial and controlled by computers

generation (jen-uh-RAY-shuhn)—all the members of a group of people or creatures born around the same time

league (LEEG)—a group of people with a common interest, such as a criminal organization

paralyze (PAY-ruh-lize)—to cause a loss of the ability to control the muscles

politics (POL-uh-tiks)—the art or science of governing a city, state, or country

tentacle (TEN-tuh-kuhl)—a long, armlike body part some animals use to touch, grab, or smell

venom (VEN-uhm)—a poisonous liquid that is injected into prey

READ MORE

Barr, Steve. *1–2–3 Draw Cartoon Aliens and Space Stuff: A Step-by-Step Guide.* 1–2–3 Draw. Cincinnati: Peel Productions, 2003.

Baugh, Bryan. *Zap!: How to Draw Fantastic Sci-Fi Comics.* New York: Watson-Guptill, 2006.

Cook, Janet and Judy Tatchell. *How to Draw Robots and Aliens.* London: Usborne Books, 2006.

INTERNET SITES

FactHound offers a safe, fun way to find Internet sites related to this book. All of the sites on FactHound have been researched by our staff.

Here's how:
1. Visit *www.facthound.com*
2. Choose your grade level.
3. Type in this book ID code **1429600756** for age-appropriate sites. You may also browse subjects by clicking on letters, or by clicking on pictures and words.
4. Click on the **Fetch It** button.

FactHound will fetch the best sites for you!

31

INDEX